Make your readers curious

Dooby's Random Factoids! ™

Did you know that a chicken once lived for a year and a half without a head?!

© Dooby Corp. Ltd

Who are these two??

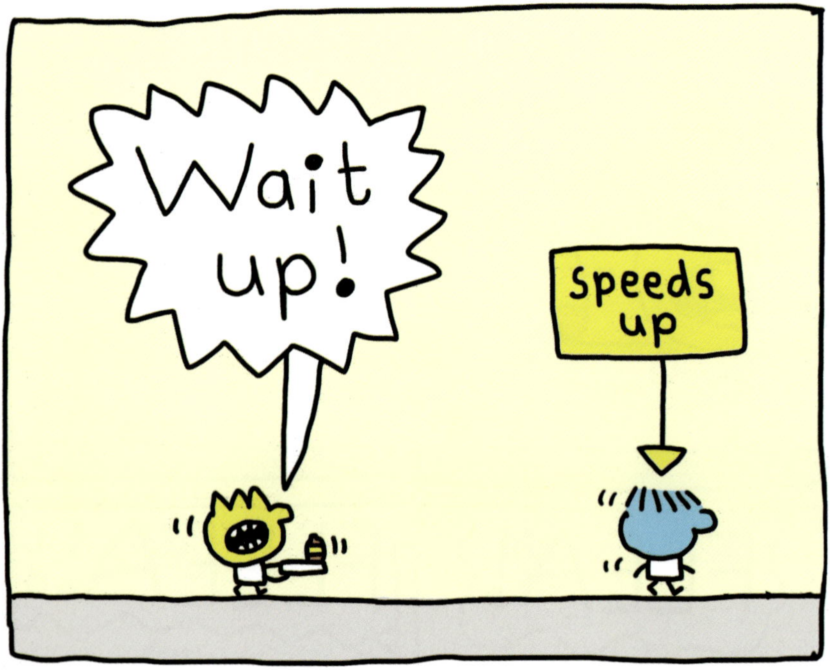
Wait up!
Speeds up

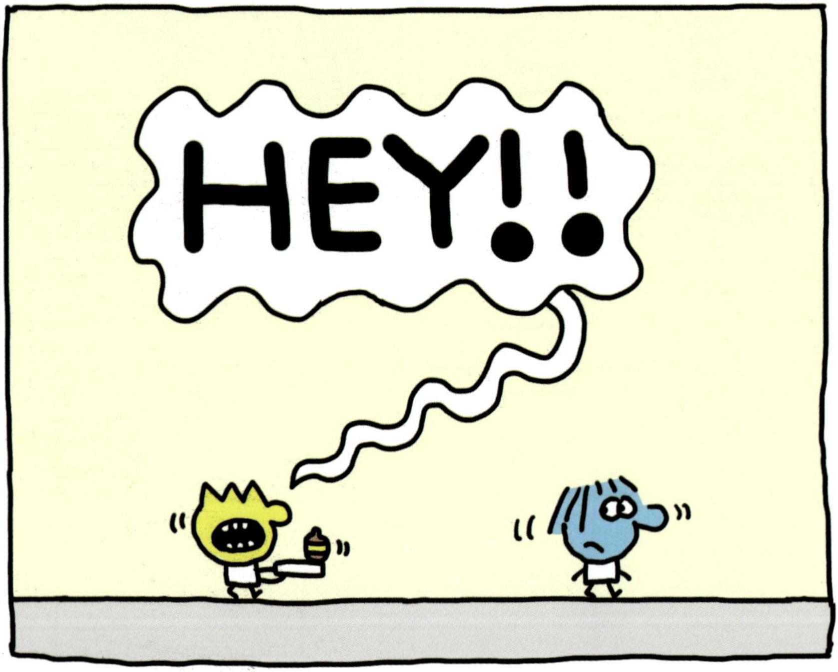
HEY!!

Well, you know the nice little bookshop in town?
Yeah...
It sold seven copies!!
...

Books are better than phones

Why people get addicted to their phones

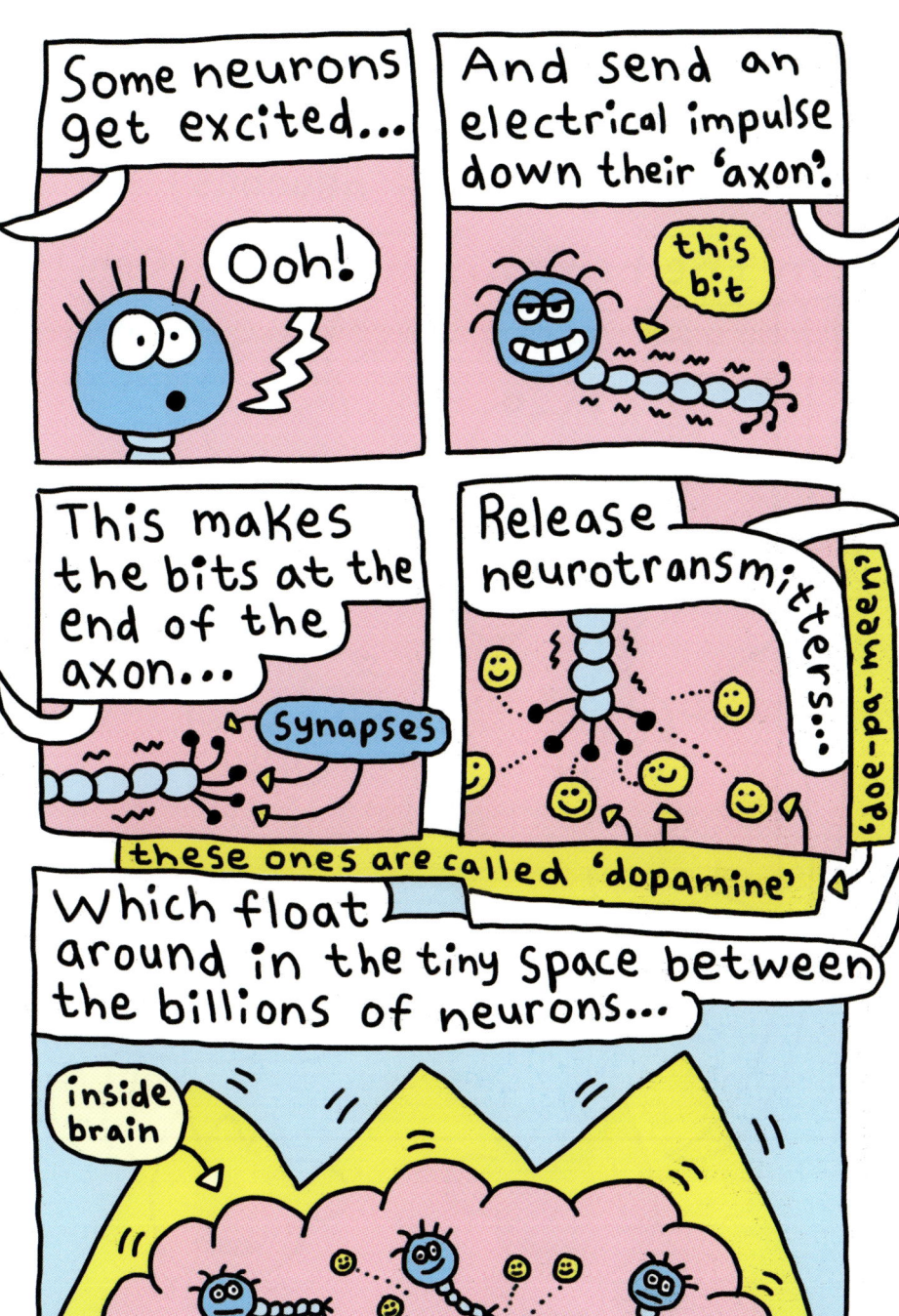

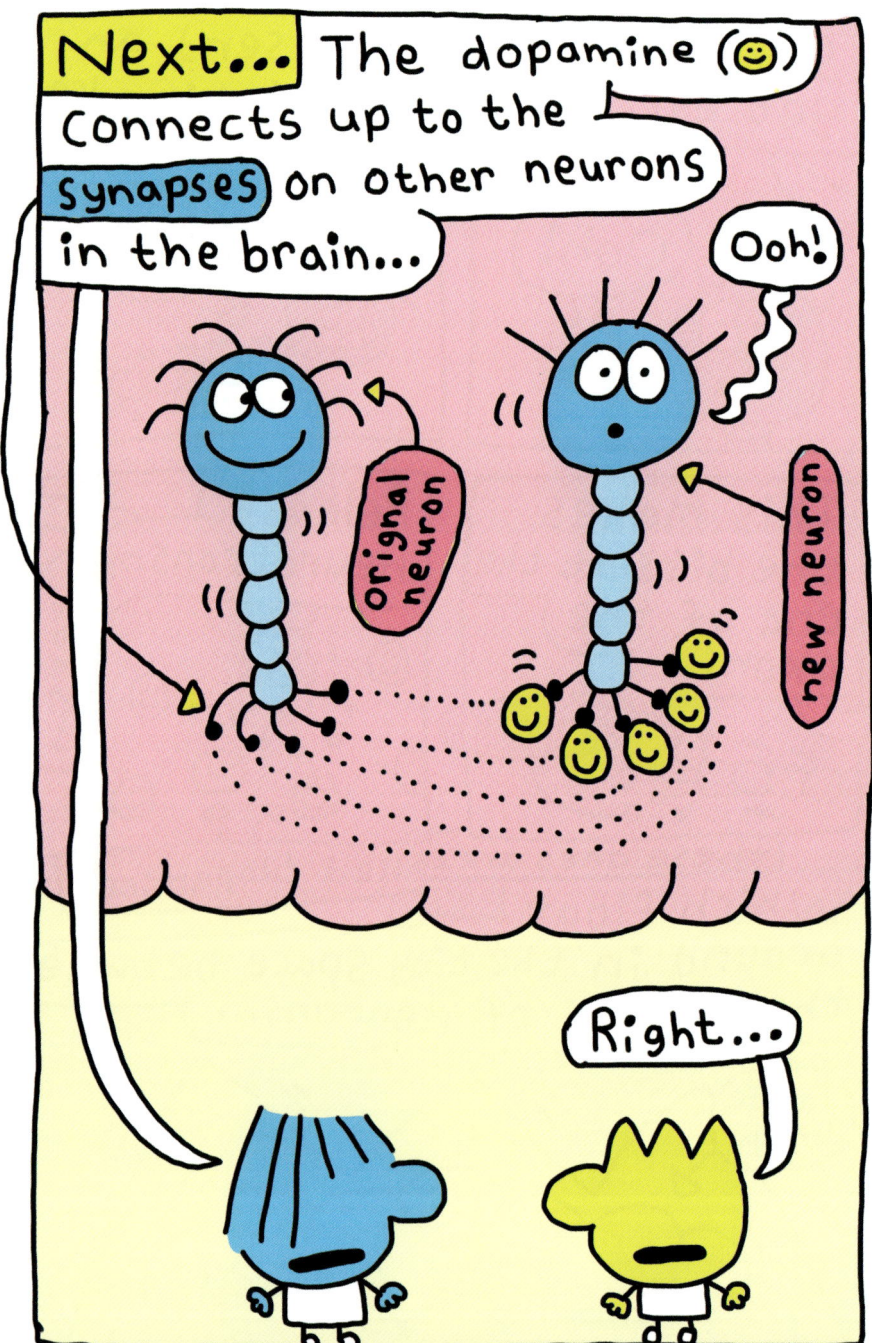

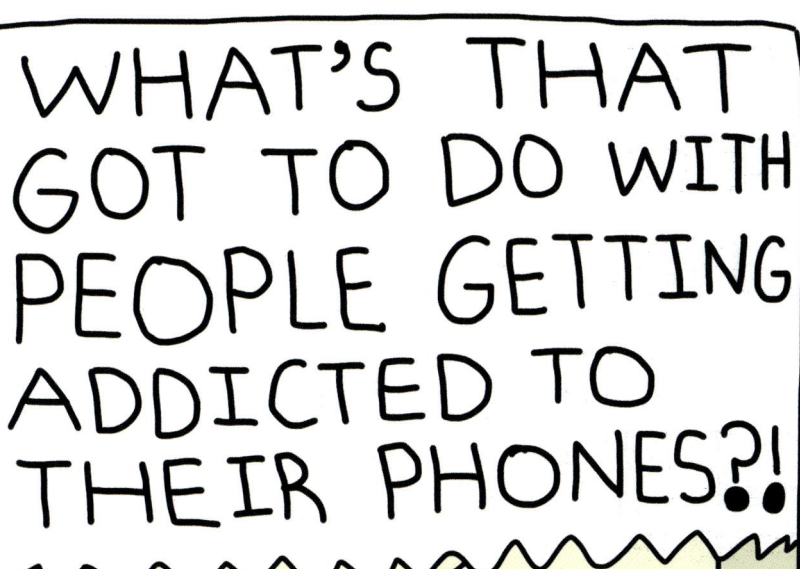

Dooby's Random Factoids! ™

One in eighteen people have three nipples!

Wait, isn't he on the front cover?

Dooby's Random Factoids! ™

FLEA'S BIG IDEA:

Let's completely copy 'Dooby's Random Factoids'!!

Erm...

I thought we were sticking with books?

Going viral isn't the only viral thing

So...
This is the common cold virus...
Hi!
Would be way, way smaller than this dot in real life.
It's made out of two parts. Let's call them...
part 1
&
part 2
Wow, you're so imaginative.
voice back to normal

Now, when someone with a cold sneezes, millions of these virus particles shoot into the air...

ATCHOO!

And if you're unlucky enough to be standing nearby, a few of them might get breathed up your nostrils.

The News

GENIUS KID CURES COLD

Gets given a billion pounds and medal & everyone agrees he's amazing and the best.

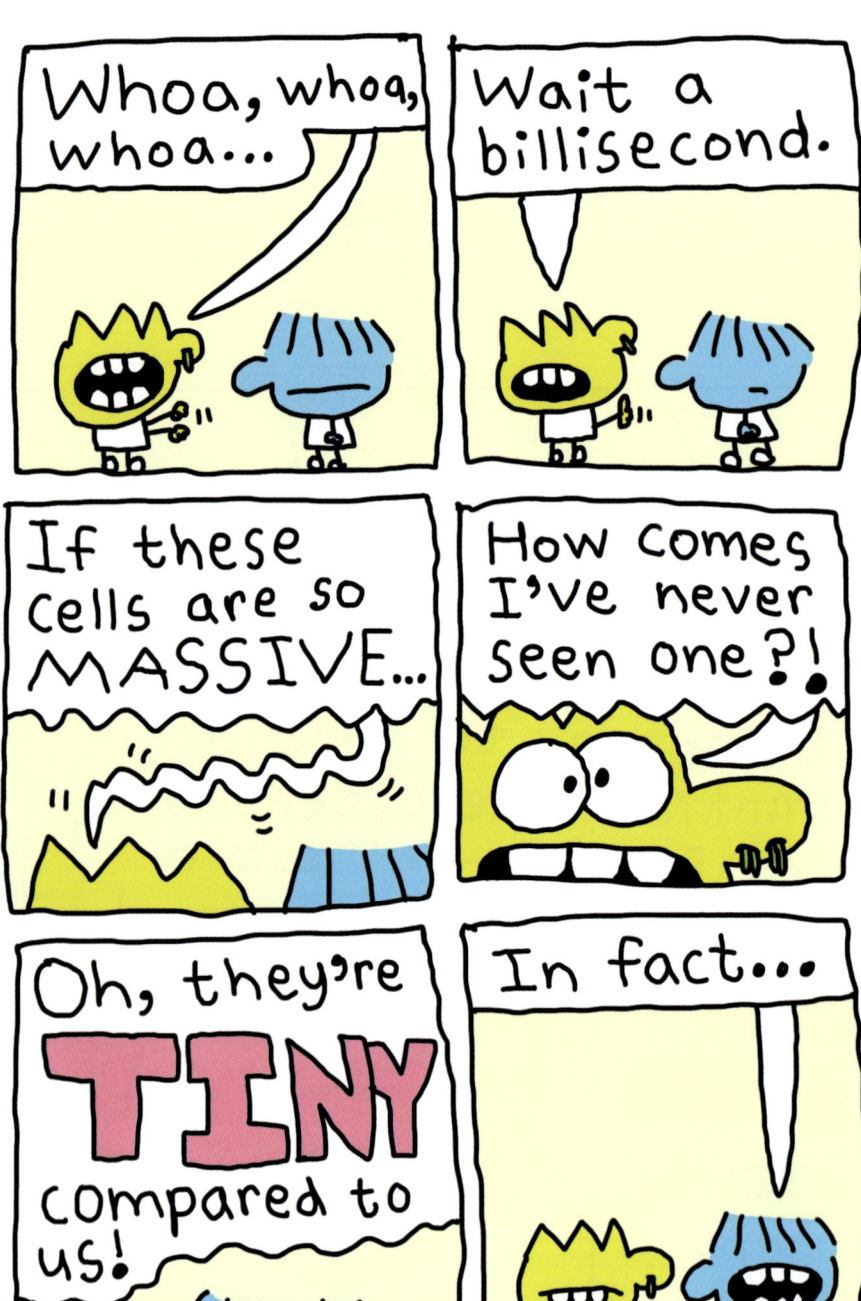

"We're about **TEN MILLION** times bigger than the average virus!!"

ANYWAY... Once the virus is up your nostril...

Hee, hee, hee!

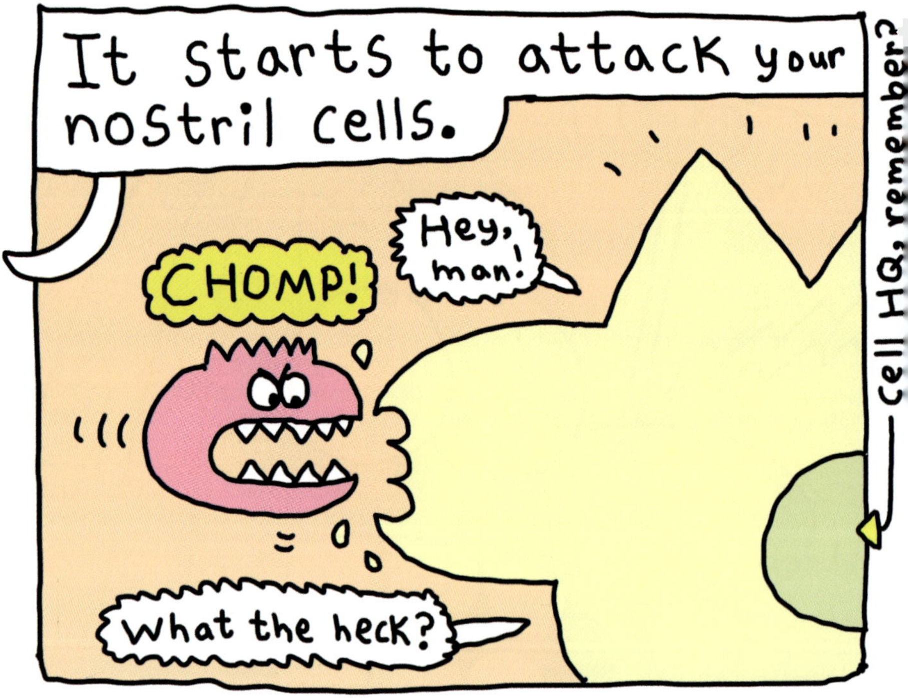

It starts to attack your nostril cells.

CHOMP!

Hey, man!

what the heck?

← cell HQ, remember?

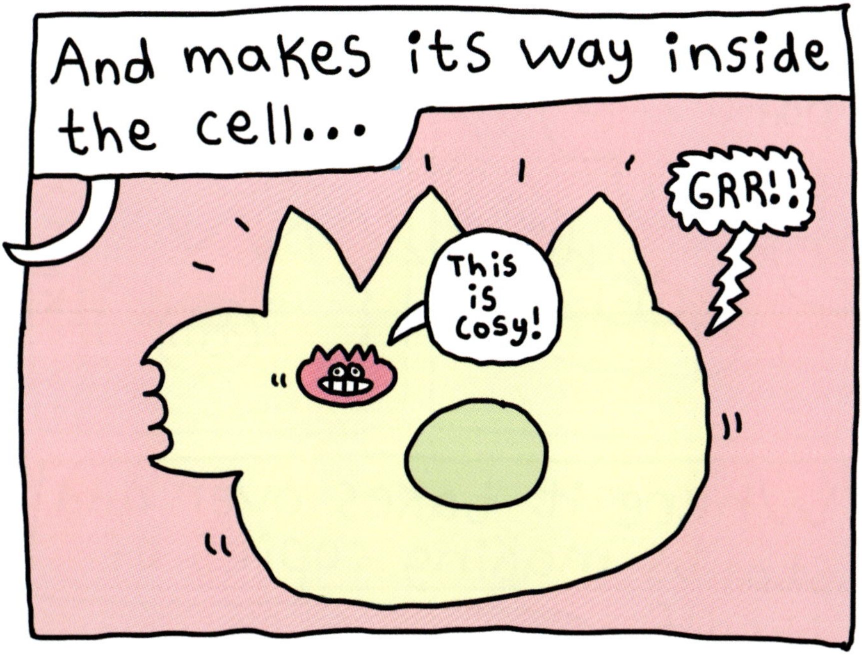

And makes its way inside the cell...

"This is cosy!"

GRR!!

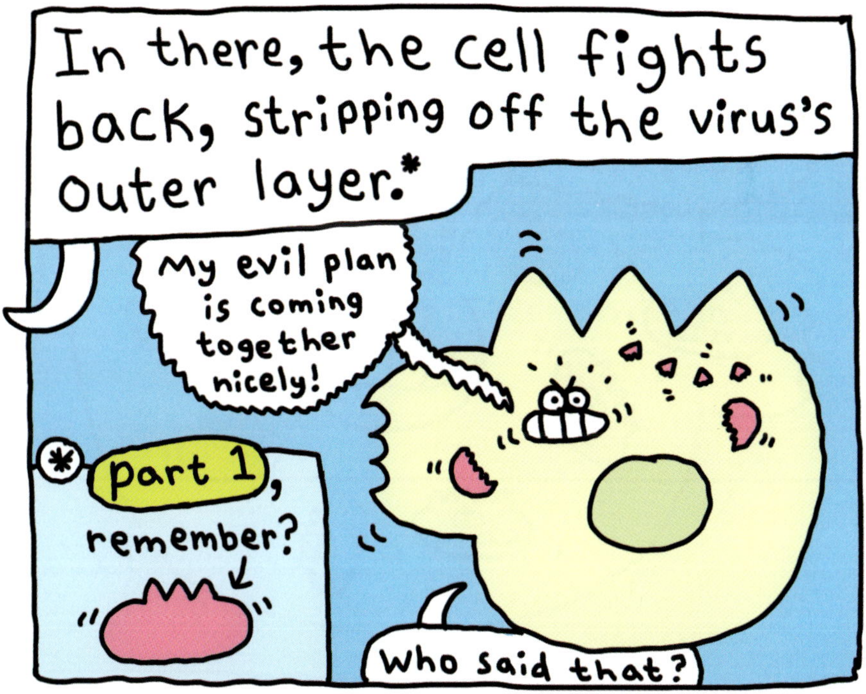

In there, the cell fights back, stripping off the virus's outer layer.*

"My evil plan is coming together nicely!"

* part 1, remember?

"Who said that?"

So...
Sometimes the cell is completely destroyed...
And all the new virus particles are released...
Free to infect even more cells.
CHOMP!
CHOMP!
CHOMP, my children, CHOMP!
CHOMP!

A quick trip to heaven

ties in with insect theme

How to kill the chompers

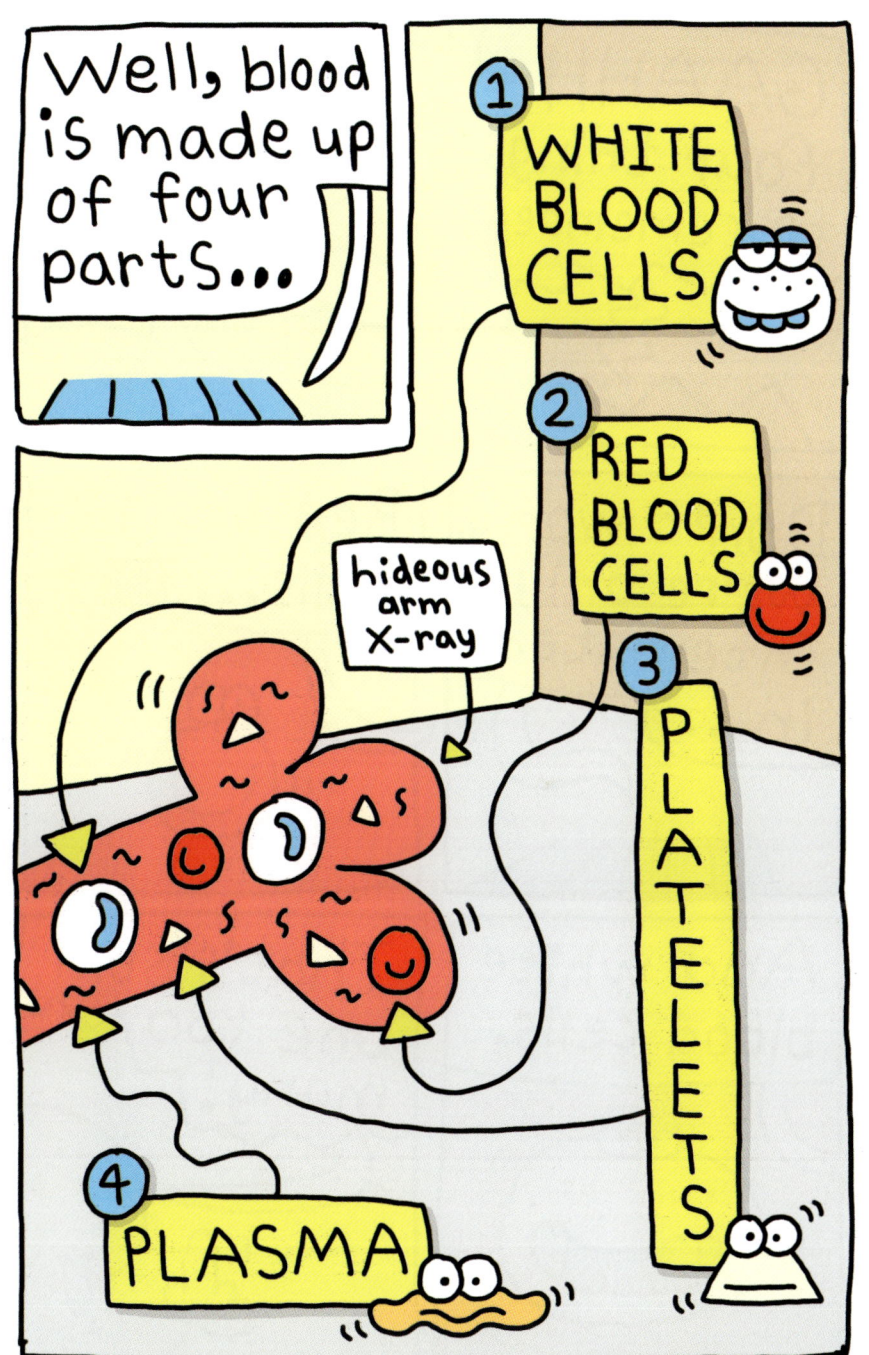

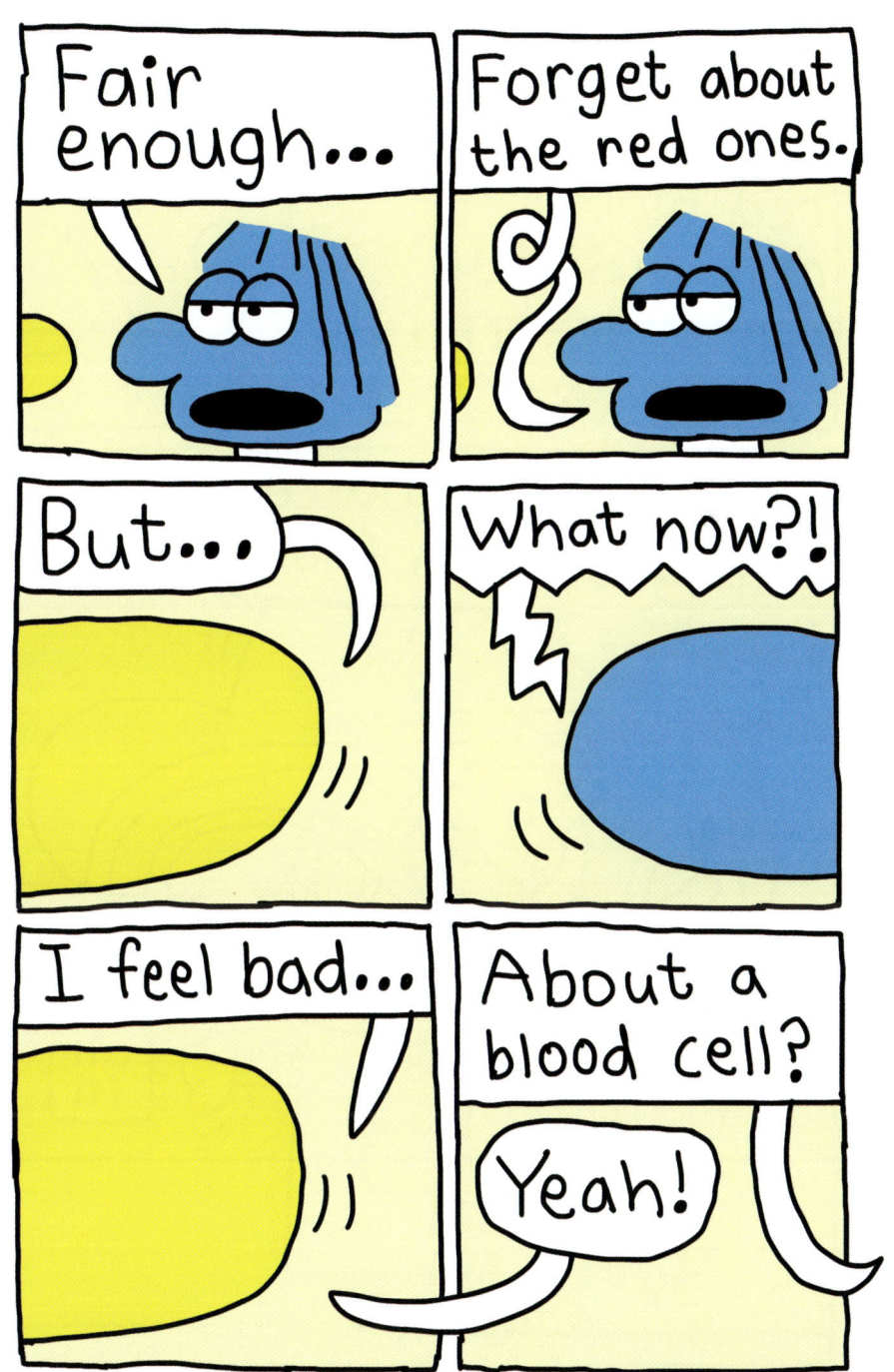

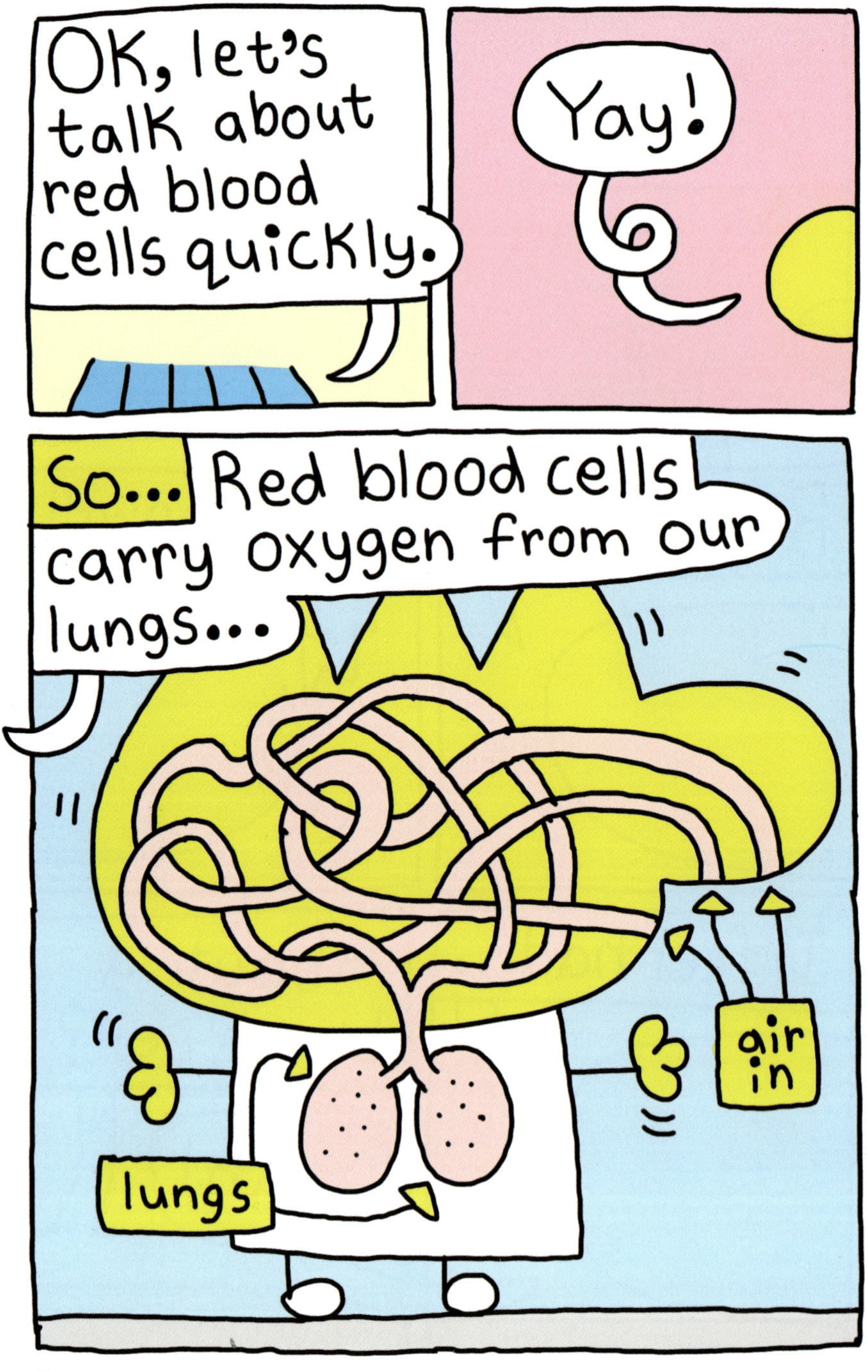

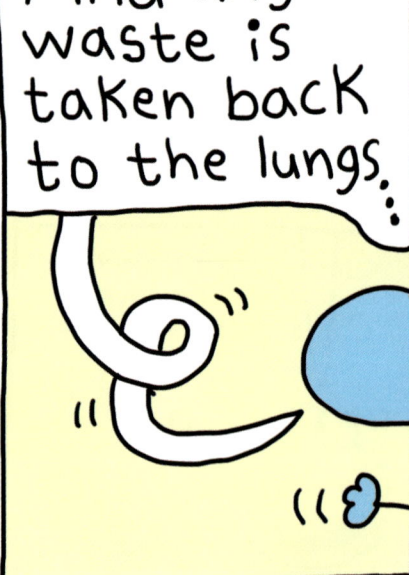

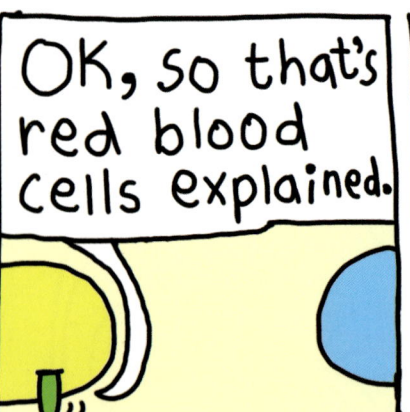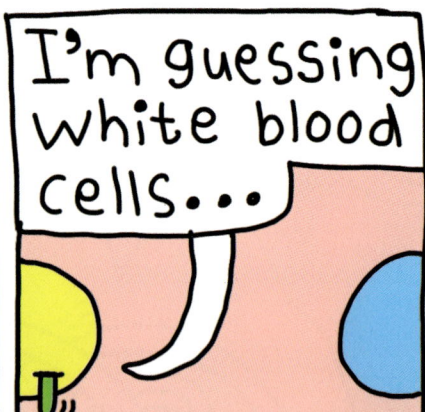

*pronounced 'sigh-toe-kines'

Cytokines are like messengers. They tell the rest of your body it's been invaded by a virus...

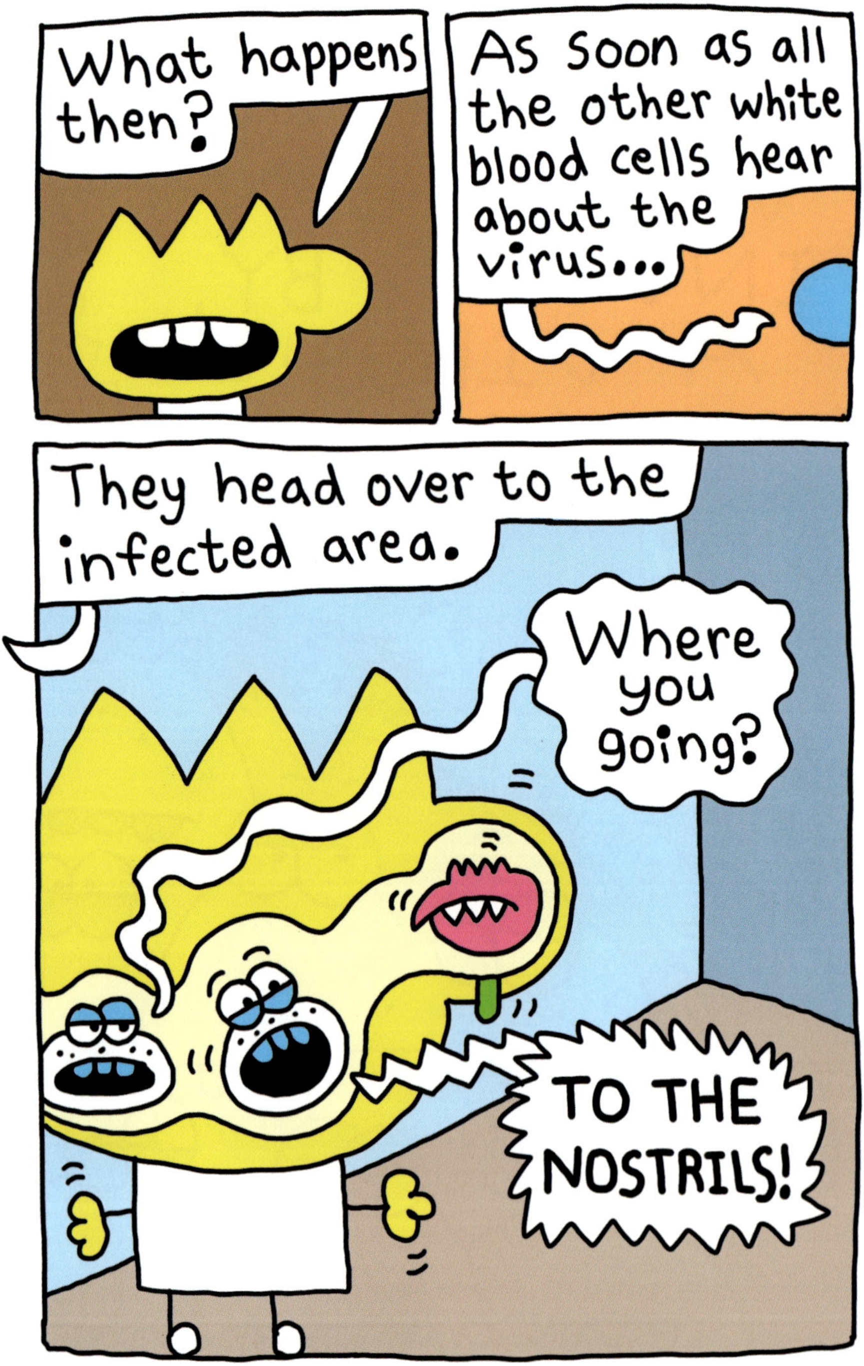

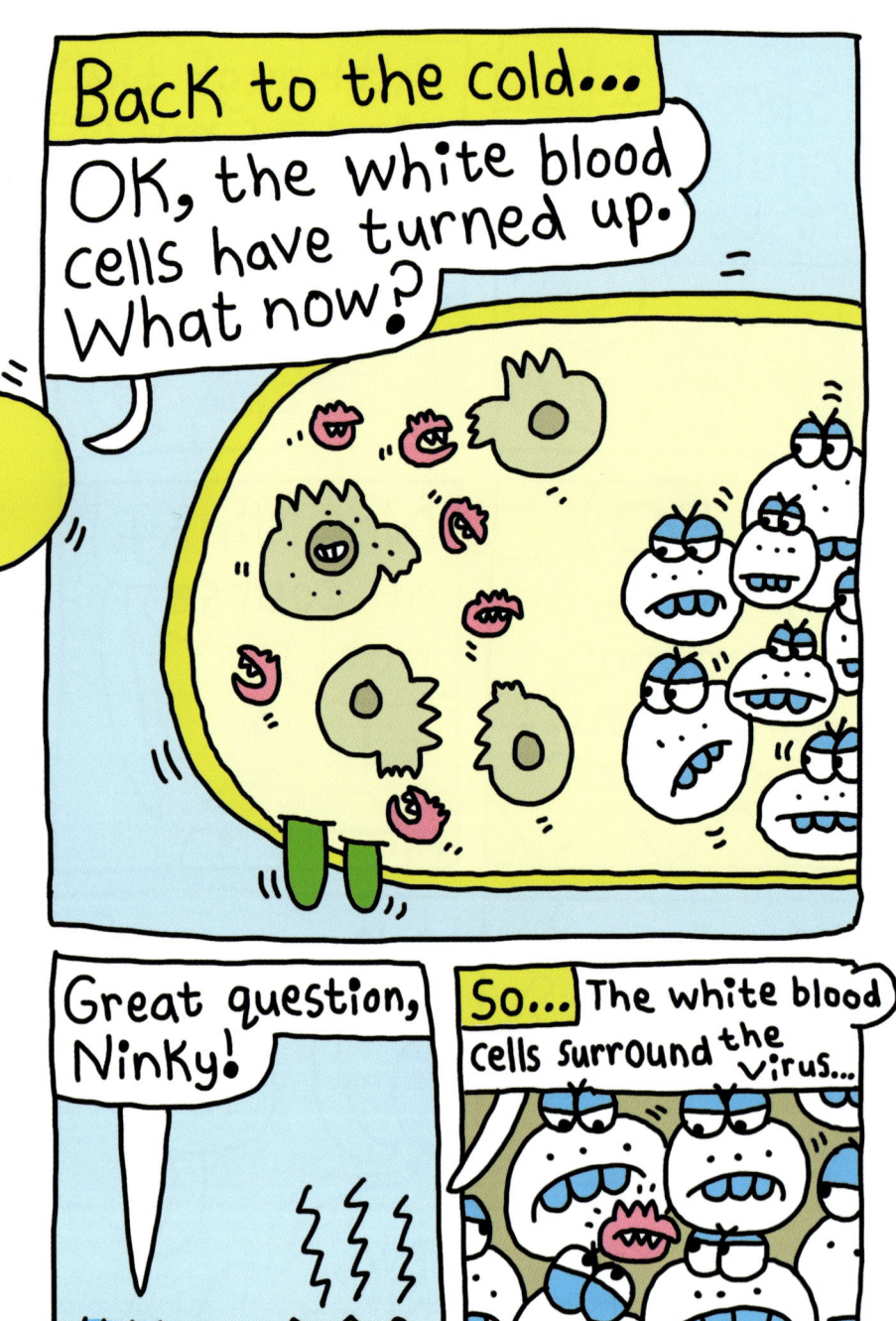

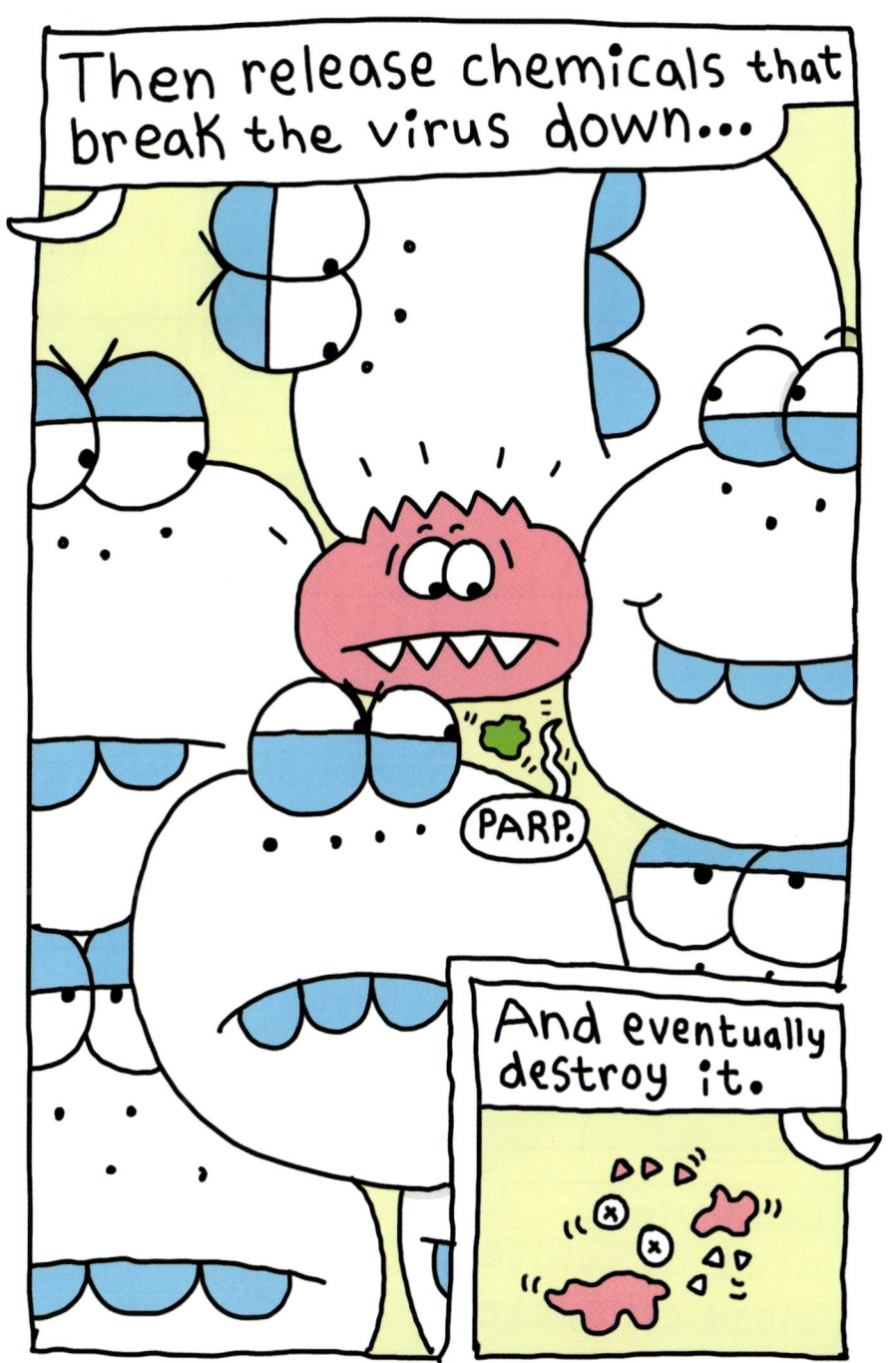

Dooby's Random Factoids! ™

Pine trees can tell if it's about to rain.

© Dooby Corp. Ltd

↑ bit random

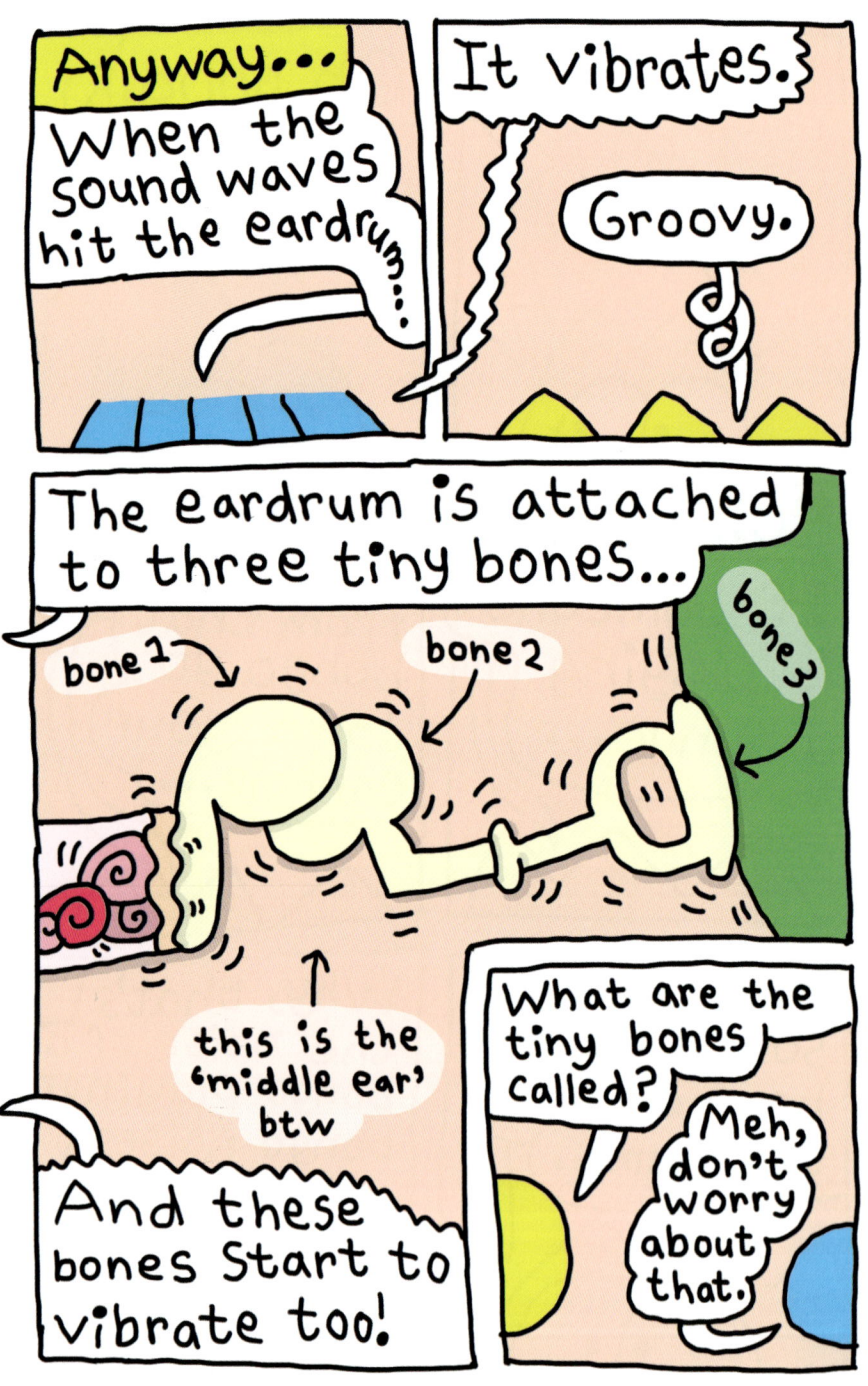

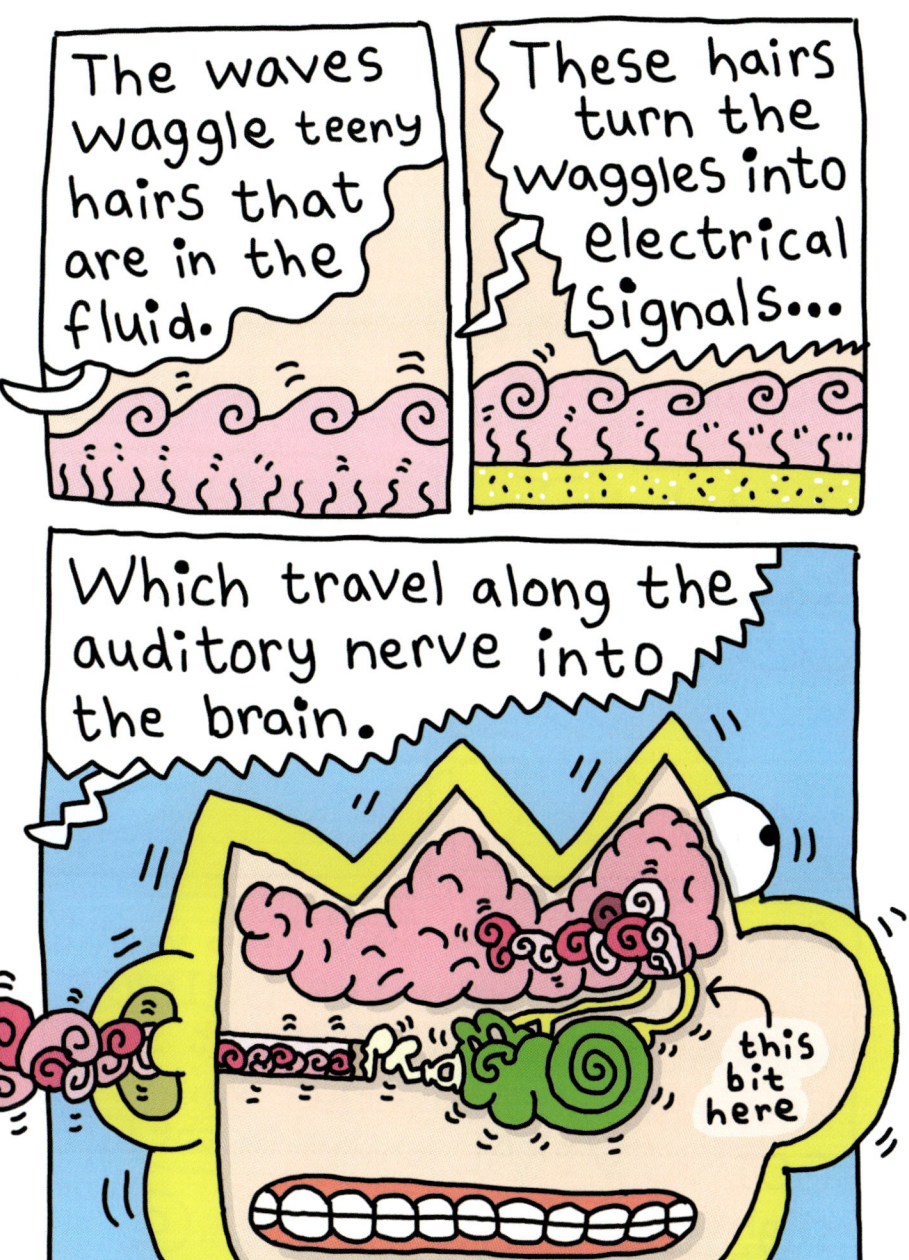

So that's how a word like 'squee' gets from my mouth to your brain, eh?

I told you not to say that word!!

I didn't say it...

I said 'a word <u>like</u> "squee"'!

GRR!!

Anyway, you said this would tie together with the GOING VIRAL thing. But I don't see how this ties together with the GOING VIRAL thing in the slightest.

How hearing annoying words like 'squee' is connected to stuff going viral

"In this lesson, I'm going to explain to you how hearing stuff is connected to going viral."

"GET ON WITH IT!!!"